Also by Chris Stroffolino

Light As A Fetter (Situations, 1997)
Cusps (Aerial/Edge, 1995)
Oops (Pavement Saw, 1994)
Oops (backyard, 1991)
Incidents (Iniquity Press, 1990)

STEALER'S WHEEL

STEALER'S WHEEL

Chris Stroffolino

lingo books

Hard Press, Inc. 1999

Some of these poems (or earlier versions thereof) have previously appeared in: *American Letters & Commentary, American Poetry Review, An Anthology of New (American) Poets, Antenym , Apex of the M, Avec, The Baffler, Break To Open, B City, CB, Combo, Compound Eye, Downtown Brooklyn, Explosive, First Intensity, Gare du Nord, The Germ, The Gertrude Stein Awards In Innovative Writing 1994-1995, Happy Genius, The Impercipient, Juxta, Letterbox, Key Satch(el), lingo, The Little Magazine, Lower Limit Speech, Make Room For Dada, Mass Ave., New American Writing, Object, Outpost Entropy, Pavement Saw, Phoebe, Poetry New York, Talisman, Texture,Tinfish, Washington Review,* and *We.*

Cover art: Grace Hartigan & Rex Stevens,
Stealer's Wheel #1, Watercolor on paper, 24 x 18 in., 1998
Cover design: Jonathan Gams
Typeset by Chad Odefey
Copyright © 1999 Chris Stroffolino
Published in the United States by
Hard Press, Inc.,
a non-profit organization:
P.O. Box 184
West Stockbridge, MA 01266
ISBN 1-889097-23-3

In Memory of my Mother, Susan Marie Hartman
(June 18, 1942–May 13, 1992)

Contents

I.

Past Control	15
Forecast of Characters	16
Brief Layover	18
As from a Distance	20
AZB of Reading	22
Song You Can't Shake Out	24
Community Vices	26
The Comedy of It All	27
Via Negativa	29
Society's Child	30
Monday Nite Garbage	31
Nature Tampered Ego Berating Beauty	34
Illegal Smile	36
Later the Same Day	37

II.

The Color of the Colorwheel	41
Drinking Andy Warhol	43
Stealer's Wheel	45
When Depth Becomes Vice	53
$18\,^{1}/_{2}$ Minute Gap	54
Over and Over	55
100% Beside Myself	56
The Shape I'm In	57
Reparations, Preparations	58
We Cancel Each Other Out in Prose	60

III.

Lingua Franca	65
Three Poems for Laura Moriarty	67
Sirhan Sirhan	69
Rain Parade	70
Now that It's April and January Is Back in America	72
Things To Do with Fire	74
Things To Do After All Hell's Broken Lose	76
For M.	77
The Verdict	78
My Daughter Would Be a Novelist	80
Allowance Money that Is Death to You	81
Hope for the Wicked	82
Fish Story	83

IV.

Flattened Until Dishevelled	87
Fragile Blonde	89
Professions of Faith	90
An Infantilization of Infinity	92
Law of Diminishing Returns	95
For Kurt Cobain	96
Partly Claudia	98
Storm Cloud Above the Swimming Pool	102
Functional Literacy (Disability Records)	103
Party Line Graffiti	104
Food for Money, Love for Thought	108

Past Control

I know why the caged past sings. I don't know if.
The subject matter is not so much the relationship
As the terms. We can only change the relationship
By changing the terms. The urge (for clean breaks)
Brakes for pedestrians too proud to be passengers
Unless they're also the drivers whose head
They hold a gun to from the perspective
Of that head, a history teacher we've left behind
Or health teacher we were banished from
Only ages ago.

Trying the objection that this may be
Entertaining at the expense of health
Without falling back on the old "reality is
For those who can't handle drugs" stand-by
In which entreaties come in the form of
Accusations always. But what can you do
When you feel situationless if not paint
A picture of the places you couldn't reject
Were you not in them as the present traps
The past and leaves just enough airholes
So it's always possible it sings

But who can hear? I could, did not the silencer
Make an awful racket as it falls from the gun
And the driver, startled, crashes into the
Passenger, as if they won't become one until
The immune pedestrian pronounces them dead
Before arrival and that may be why we've
Been known to play taps regardless of what we're
'Really' doing down there in the headlines of dreams.

Forecast of Characters

To hide nothing, but the more you say the more
You hide. I smell a rat, the rat of disinfectant.
It chases its tail to mimic me, though you'd
Never guess by its shadow, the light of its shadow,
What psyche does to chronos, what worlds open up
Between words, the vows I would've eaten had I made
Time the neon sign over the drugstore that has
Gathered us together.

The benevolence of the unknown opens up like
A repentant cop-out. We gaze at the mess as if
We've made it. If we didn't think we made it
We wouldn't see it as a mess. Meeting in a fog,
The fog of meeting. Try it on a clear day, a day
That struggles to stay clear, the sun dodging
The clouds that would burn its wings & if the
Opposite's not true, or fashionably false, a need
For time to sort things out meets the fear you're
Bored in solitude as we're swept away by yet another
Pawnshop. Naked, without a body. To mind not knowing
What it's missing. The riddle pathos causes, curses.

Undiluted by your genderlessness, they won't believe
You're for real, but you'll think they're for real
Just so you don't have to believe you are. This is
Called friendship. As if a single man looks at
A woman as a married man looks at death, oh warehouse
That doesn't exist until ransacked! How it takes two...

To take a toll, a pulse, to intercept the aspirin
For all the times the uptight action is best so extremes
Go their merry way like clothes to an outgrown shop
Which becomes a laundrymat. Listen to what is many
But seems like one while you still can, cut the roots

Into characters because what else are you going to do
In a cave with a friend you don't know is your friend
Just yet and be sure to make where you got it from
Where I got it from (He guards his gold). Now raise
Your hands if you think you're growing up too slow.
No takers? "Knowing where I am's a nice place to visist
But..."

One more time and I'll have you stay after and write
"It can happen here" a thousand times in stage blood,
The red car of black coffee. The early morning which
Sheds no light on the ends of night and people always
Emerging from opposite ends of the cloud they put on
A pedastal to balance the bandaid that someday will
Grow up to be a real wound, no strings attached
(just a lot of salespeople standing around trying to make
you feel guilty until proven customer, costumer).
What yesterday has to do with it without losing its
Identity in the product, the pocket calculator of
Consciousness that lets you cry so obviously flawed
No one will yell at us for making it seem to beg
Love to trope. Meet me out back. I'll promise...
I can do it in my sleep. Only in my sleep.

Brief Layover

To solve the problem of idealism
do you kick it out to invite it in
(as if anonymity is a way to offend
those overeducated by default
and everything else is conjecture too)?

The word 'human' as an unmoved mover
(as if you are only present neither here
nor there, a trap that tries and tries
to call off the cause-effect relationship
we have with ourselves as others)

Only as petty as the feelings which accompany
things swept under the sofa in the room of
ostensibly neat solitude torn between the
activity that is dilemma and the dilemma....

A child called 'activity' grows up differently
than one called 'dilemma.' Someone shows you
a picture of how silly you look trying
to be objective about it. And no one has
to decide that determinism is utterly wrong
in the womb we assume
for all the good extremities do.

If indeed the body is to praise
what the mind is to blame, you can lose it
remembering your name as easily as by forgetting
all observers erased by the rose-colored glasses
of pessimism they find on their face
once the urge to scratch eclipses the task at hand
become reified by a present not elusive enough
to help life, that parrot, along in its descent
as water pretends to be other to fall for water

for all the times it doesn't feel like a lie
to tell of where I come from. The pleasures
of the harbour, of the text seen as the harbour,
a brief layover in the activity not seen as dilemma,
without the you, a bug the skeptic who fashions
himself presence can't work out of the system
in which insiders surely look down on outsiders
now that we've rid ourselves of the urge
to get things out of the way
until one wave hits and another hit waves.

As from a Distance

It's not so bad to live as if between two poles.
Nor is it so bad to live as one, or both,
Of the poles another lives as if between.
Nor will I say it's better or worse
To watch the game as from a distance,
To watch those who only watch it
Until you, becoming it, take them with you.
And if you don't, there's no need for
Theatrical loss–said the poem to the play–
In this case I am a question I beg...

Stories of those who took a chance that paid off
Seduce you the first time, but will they
Hold up under Repeated Readings? Will you?
You who want to see but not to be
The people who came in and out
Of your life like books back when having all
The weather in the world was Greek to you
And there were no bookstores but libraries
More often closed when you're open
And open when you're closed

So individuals rose in value
And TVs tore down theatres
And busses divided themselves
Into the cars with which the century
Would speed to its close like the book
In the lap of someone who doesn't
Like being preached to, the book
You cannot chose to be read by
Even if you must seduce the food
In your freezer as much as a shoplifter
In her toy supermarket, grateful
For a cold day in spring so she

Doesn't feel she's missing anything
In not straying from the isolation chamber
Without which the world would be
Lazy and/or carefree, only a hybrid
If a hybrid can do away with
The categories she sees it before.

AZB of Reading

Picture the love which is only physical
Carrying on (a conversation) with the
Love which is in no way physical.
You best picture some one who doesn't
Do windows unless they feel like frames,
The practicality as easy as AZB
Against the backdroplessness of chronology
You once called meaning back when we
Sided with meaning so much we never met.

"I for one have only taken human form
To be convincing," said the savior,
A small town in SE Pennsylvania dying
To give birth to it, dying in advance for
The sins we have to go out of way to
Commit for his sweet sake. Outside, the wind
And rain sang its siren song and hands
Were seen stealing from our heads to
Make sure the silly putty was on straight
So we couldn't hear the world for the
Mickey Mouse club Psychomachia
We're known to see it as still.

The candy sampler radio casts itself
As ID opposite the straightman of School,
TV, mean from too many years spent
Occupying the mean which deduces Eden
From the Sahara meanwhile back in
The zeitgeist where nothing is trapped
But that which thinks it's free
And nothing's life but that which
Can't be picked up, though foolproof
As a recipe and convincingly human
As a Pentagon frankly sick of sitting
At the head of the round table of

Your soul shopping for the camera
With which to photograph its cameralessness.

So picture the unforeseen as the airholes
In the jar of memory we flicker in,
The unforeseen done justice to accidentally
At best, the judge never understanding,
The case thrown out by the opposite of
An earthquake (as the Governor's urge
to crack down on crime is seen moving
to the right). Sure decisions are made
Only when they come up and this may be the
Biggest blizzard of shivering since trains
Of thought first derailed leaves of grass,
Chaotic as an urge for order, yet aware
That a differing mood may make out in such
Shivering the figures I can't see for
The haze which keeps me company until
The weekend approaches refusing to die
Unless it takes the week with it,
Not that it has it to lose.

Song You Can't Shake Out

Now the denial of activity seems embraced,
But I am not nostalgic for my last brushes
With what goes by too many aliases for
Its authenticity not to be in severe question
In wit and wartime the goal to weave
Without being a weaver or a web
Unless it's easier to see the weaver
In the web than in the weaving soul
Breath erects a wall around
So no coffin is immortal

Just because the book is long doesn't mean
You can't stay on one page all night.
"We muscles know how to be untensed
if only you listened for once...but you
got caught up in the ecstacy of having found
inside you voices as if the idea of water
could quench." It's the conscience salesmen,
Bar the door. Agency floats. Sean calls....

We choose our friends as we choose to leave
The window open. Not so much the open
And shut case, same day surgery, as the
Song of solitude it takes two to jam on
As the bottom falls out the way what screams
From the silent center makes the first move
By telling me to make it
The presence which keeps us warm

Nothing wrong with cozy,
with yelling at yourself for feeling vaguely fine
Yelling at yourself to feel more precise,
Yelling become telling, telling become
Touching and I can't tell the blinker

From the blink so I must be in a hole this thick
("If you hate yourself for rejecting
an act of violence, you didn't reject it")
To squander doubt on the mundane
So the free meet the free in the free
While the urge to lose count gets its 15 minutes
And someone surely has my number
And can see through the soliloquys
So there's no throng to do but
Accept her suspensions because bodies
Are not stories or theories about bodies
And, as the threshold pauses to take
A picture of itself that will never come out
Like a deed in the wash, I have to like you
Enough to want to argue with you to love you
Enough to feel no need to.

Community Vices

The desire to place yourself
in a sink-or-swim scenario
on deck the decision boat
is but pragmatic in the oatmeal light
of the interpreters I've been "known"
to mistake for the sun.

The seeds that live in the plants
strain toward the disk of the sun
which, full of itself, spills from
the frame of fame for the sake
of selves resembling reprimands
made to break but so many bend
unlike an accident, bereft of a place
in schemes of the universe.

If we didn't look up we couldn't climb down.
The eye whose hurricane is taken as given,
if not the shiny exoskeleton of those rotten
at the core of which we spoke at the stop past Bliss,
is not in any middle a wall flower couldn't occupy
so you don't have to except me to accept me
a song which couldn't be about you
were I not seen singing it for my supper.

But the seeming wake-up call
seen as the putting-to-sleep
is but the spectacles we wore
out of fear of being blinded by
the community we turned our back on
when we turned our back on selves.
Then the flag points towards its own
destruction, its burning mystery
and on that snake you
might say I build my church.

The Comedy of It All
for Peter Gizzi

The civilization we can save is the one we must perform.
So let's love the lack the artist becomes in fulfilling
the prophecy whose parody is God and then teleology.
Now you are entering a train on which no baggage
is permitted, not even a ticket; far less the mind
that can not be nourished without biting the eyes that feed it,
the vased eyes uprooted from the communal heart of nothing.

A sudden awareness of emptiness upon looking in a mirror
need not destroy a night devoted to performance
after those you'd pick up the phone for are most likely asleep.
First, you must stop thinking "bandaid on the wound" everytime
someone says "truce." Then you must realize you cheat on him
not to sleep with me. For now is not the time to respond
to a tautology which would only be the universe had the airholes
not been left at the home you could never go back to
and therefore would like to see burnt along with the caboose
its engine makes of everything else due to the pressure of
the teleological rainbow we disembarked from so we could laugh at
the only thing that distinguished us from animals if we could be sure.

Why not die in possibility? Death is no closure, so don't expect
a job to save you. And lovers are like language, mediums
that become a message only when the messenger is Mexico
and then Maine, never torn between deep sanity and Spain
except when seen from the eyes painted on a totalizing train
stuck at the station where the tracks meeting at the vanishing point
are as equidistant from either of our local heresies as the blood
we can't believe is breathing in any brains but these of paper pens
behind our backs which would shut the sliver with standards
too high to be the nothing we can't help but live up to.

For we are on the road from lights and cameras to action,
running out of gas like a rabbit, gnawing at the husks of selves
to speak from the five perspectives that fight it out in
what would only be the "unintegrated personality" of the hero
were poetry suppossed to be closer to tragedy than comedy.
Plenitude is what pierces the pleasure of whining relieved
of responsibility as the waiting room invades the dissecting table
like a bull who swears it entered the china shop by default

We begrudgingly begin to enter a skyscraper someone else made
by convinving ourselves we're erecting it. It doesn't afford us
a better view. Those shadowed by it were not essential.
We are all on top and the bottom doesn't cave in.
Gravity is defied by the giddiness of a tragedy that couldn't
be moving unless what killed the characters killed the actors.
Sometimes it does. We can't find replacements. Ticket prices soar.
Specialists preside in bodies who wouldn't have an urge to brush
into each other were not government marginalized by tricks
and anger, when imagination must be a one-liner and we are all
prostitutes. Such loveliness is no more perverse than exhaling
after holding back during the performance that had pressed you
against a wall oblivious to all who'd be a real drag in person
did they not have you for an onstage audience.

Via Negativa

Seasons are either broad brushstrokes or little dots.
There is no in between. The TV is either on or off.
I'm not over my head in love yet. Or is love life?
Wriggling dusts itself on, a Nestea plunge seen as
a leap of faith. What is the time that passes
terribly slow if no one knows what time is?
What is lumber but kindling in a scorching summer?
And why is meaning such a proofless cross to carry
when you feel you make it or break it, but never both at once,
since it costs more to eat than shit, except at christmas,
as if one bad apple can spoil the whole DDT sprayed bunch
and the voice has not made the wilderness it winks in
in a myth we have to pass through, but no doubt should
edit out for the kind of network cameras we make fun of,
as if we're out of time.

We'd reject such dreams if the end were analysis, or
we can afford to flunk the final and are gamblers, all of us,
cunning in our alienation and our wonder and that cunning
is what keeps us together, as if glued to our seats so long
soon paranoia seems a vacation where once it was but a price
to be paid for the pleasure of being watched. And this is nothing
if not involved with love, though someone stole my name
and robbed theft as well and there is no drama but memory
and hope even in the hottest chicken so the zoo
can yawn in the garbage of fertility to bring is to the body

Society's Child

Static–the unchanging quality of noise.
The cacophony of the status quo propped up
by ocassional claims of subversion. Amorality
of the public domain disguised as morality
to confer upon the domestic sphere a degraded
status of Miller Time–a hangover cured
by the courtesy one wears like a badge
upon re-entering the bored meeting
in which crying like sweating is a disruption
of the progress poets pretend to know better than
even as they slum it in their own borrowed breath
or consign it to a private world which becomes
the bodily whore to the mental virgin of
the wild blue end in itself, applauded for
its triumph over teleology and its slavery to,
absorption by, normative structures
as if teleology is a bigger culprit than
the uses it has been, and continues to be, put to–
Yet just because many rivers flow into
stagnant ponds doesn't mean that
every one must. There are ends in life,
if no final, private, one. Ends that may
be seen as people in whom we define ourselves
(and place in a hierarchy unless the way we act
really believes in "free love"). If they don't
talk back in a way which can not be easily
incorporated into your own being (though they
may be incorporated into the art that exceeds
your own being like a signature), well, then,
you can acknowledge the loopholes death, God's
new clothes, gives you. And we're back to statues.

Monday Nite Garbage

1.
The things you want to hear have been talking
to the things you don't want to hear for some time,
but I've been known to say stomach and mean belly,
brain when (those who say 'mind' when they mean
'soul' say) I mean mind. So it's okay, don't rush it.
The climbers above have no paper on you
(because paper has no paper on you).

And what's beyond argument, the owl valued wise
in the lyric west because it can't see in the daylight,
pulls the plug on the not-to-be-forgotten fool
that pulls the rug out from under you.
Hatred comes in the guise of the victim to whom
hatred comes, as if you have no soul but situations
against which, allegedly in order to live, you dig
a shelter in which there's no room for error
because there's no holes for air.

The meat of the argument was you had to
be a vegetable to be a vegetarian.
We all pale before photosynthesis.
Existence does our dirty work.
You were better at history than at math
but history makers are often better at math.
You fidget for fudged gravity, getting
cold feet on "This Is Your Life" unless
it's in black and white for the sake of
those who need competition to excel,
the kind of painting you're afraid of
falling in love with at first sight.

2.
I jump from the train of skepticism
(disguised as symbolism) for the feeling
of jumping. Not that a warmer fate is more
in touch with the simple folk. I started
to stray early. What did you expect?
Awakening from fervor?

Sure, madness is the madam
in the whorehouse of the soul
but any love divorced from duty will remain
unrequited unless the desire for something
not obligatory may rise as uninhibitedly
as in the daze of old. Maybe even moreso
because of the increased running-jump
it needs to burst through the victory tape
of self-consciousness.

"I'd trade my soul in for the world if that
were not jumping from the frying pan
into the fire." But as long as some things
ugly on the outside are ugly on the inside
some pleasing on the outside can be pleasing
on the in, though most ins end up on the outs
and awareness that one doesn't notice
the scenery enough isn't enough to
make you look at it more unless there's
such an animal as a guilty glance, as has
been rumoured in these parts by someone
who demands difficulty so much it's often
the last to come and the first to leave
the parties it sees as waiting rooms,
someone who dropped out of politics
but only for political reasons.

If there's worse things than feeling pulled
from the audience on "Let's Make A Deal"
surely there's better things than it and
"You're not in the gutter if you don't care
you're in the gutter" may save the day
once again for those who have their cake
& so live to eat on a denotative level
but connotations bubble beneath (if you
have to take it too hard to take it to heart).

The painted weathermap began to chip revealing
the weather, and we're not even embracing.
Next you you know we were too busy loving
the day for its body to hear the calls of the
jealous mind this, in all probability, is.

Nature Tampered Ego Berating Beauty

To start, mark the distinction between
The singer who does it for money
And she who does it for the soul.
But neither necessarily applies to any person.
When an argument is brought down to earth
It is brought down to complexities
So, like someone running for President
Under the pretext he's trying to
Start a revolution, I must remember
You own me as I remember NBC
is loved by General Electric.

Before I got into this habit
Of accidentally dialing my own number
When I call to convince you it's not
Forgiveness I want, love was like
The language I couldn't help but be in.
Now when someone is attracted to me
By the way I'm not afraid to look at her,
I lose the nerve to say I'm using the window
She sees me through 'merely' as a mirror.

He's only been around the block
If she beats around the bush
If Freud burnt holes in the rug
Of sexuality he thought was a floor...
Fact: more women buy locks than men.
A nearby congressman (who loves
campaigning for office more than
being in it) tells me, "So if you're
A man and don't buy a pick, you might
As well be buying a lock...unless
You don't expect your girlfriend to
help you find someone to cheat on her with."

I guess he's right if "all roads lead to Rome"
Means you have to take every road to get to Rome.
To him, I go the wrong way down a two way street
As if there ever was a time we weren't making love
For a reason. To him, no doubt, I've come from
That stunted world where forgiving the temptress
Is yielding to the temptation while darkness
Falls like priests robes over the candle
That dies burning holes in them,

Where cocktail parties are hair salons
And electrons loiter in the sweatshop
Of the heart, looking with fear into
The eyes of she who soothes what I follow,
Neither lethal nor legal. If I told him
"If you wouldn't have lied you couldn't
have laughed" would he say
"But just because you're ruined
Doesn't mean you're right" or would
He pretend he didn't hear, afraid
He wouldn't get my vote?

A bridge falls through its cracks
And those who buy a suit to land the job
That pays for it are too corrupt to love
But not corrupt enough to survive.
But why should we tamper with a success
That may rot if we don't tamper with it?

Illegal Smile

To leave America behind with the lightning
that doesn't last long enough to meet
the demands of time, a player you can
only meet by working, puts us in the
driver's seat of cars which don't exist
because the fact we don't work on assembly lines
no longer means laziness except to those who
not only try their best to make you feel guilty
for making love on welfare but also do
their 'best' to be the anchors on which your
emotionalized attention must moor (since
surely the only reason you're at sea is you're
a stowaway and surely swimming rivers
might as well be walking on water in El Salvador
where there is no war no more but the peace
in which property is poverty in a minor key
between the lines of a newspaper like the prison
bars poetry tries to bolt from only to get
accused of imperialism and isolationism
in the lusty process) and you're back in the rain
in which what you saved is playing
possum (or so you hope) as you dreamt
that midnight came and pulled you from the top
of the burning ladder into the next day
as a theme of hailstones hurled
at cabbies in a walking city.

Later the Same Day
for Pam Rehm

To risk isolation, enact a stupidity,
To plant a sick seed in hopes of making
The harvest healing. I think it's possible
I wouldn't be thinking now did I not
Have the memory of some unthinking time
To think about, something to explain, defend
Rescue or attack, correct, make light of.

It doesn't have to be dark for there to be
Something to make light of. There need be
No contrast when the past becomes bitter
In memory to make the present better...
But I don't want to be so busy being a
Poet's poet that I forget to be a poet,
I mean person, sometimes sexless, perhaps
More sexless when not genderless,
More natural when human and closer to you
When closest myself to free pleasure
From the taint of compromise,
A kind of injoke of temperance.

There's only a time to plant and a time
To reap when there's no guarantee the words
That seem like sure thumbs to me will seem so
When you write, as if I know no special place
But my desk, my hard drive, as I retreat
To wonder where the hell you are and passion
Pricks up its ears like a dog the mayor
Of the city under seige leaves stranded in
Its not-so-secret suburban home but the
Election was so fixed it gave birth to
Nothing but that which has
No beginning or end

which I love until I should
until shouldn't dies killing should
and I'm happy to be back beyond
happiness and sadness again
and the ends that only justify the means
if the ends are now where only mistakes
can make the best of mistakes
and the way matters more than the place
even if all the food goes to the same place
even if only for affirmative action reasons.

II

The Color of the Colorwheel

When abstracting green from grass
is no easier than abstracting it from envy
and the yellow and blue that stood behind it
are snatched like crutches to see if it stands
on its own two legs, colorless as the colorwheel,
the wheelchair of legacy sitting in for the feet.
This is not a matter of drought, of grass
turned brown, but of what keeps the topsoil
from eroding, the common ground that's left
what dollars share with lettuce in the lurch
as long as we're so green we see brown as red.

On a day as bright as a green light at night,
We travel. If red has to pass through brown
to get to green, we are only on a wild goose chase
if we are wild geese. And even if you must pass
through something like Canada to get from
the USA to Cuba, we all know what the odds are
of a Slav being able to communicate with a Thai
without knowing English. Green is not so much
a lingua franca as Brown is. A graduate student
with a T.A. is to reddish-green what a teacher
who refuses to learn from her students
is to brown.

One who could be praised as easily as blamed
for not seeing the trees for the forest sees
the brown lights of christmas. The more one sees
green and red where once one saw brown
the less likely one is to have something to hide.
I thought this table had a lot to hide until
I noticed the various shades of brown.
The darker shades are more likely purple-yellow
than blue-orange. Red-green is more balanced

than purple-yellow, but it's neck-and-neck
with blue-orange. Purple-yellow is
the more likely third party candidate

The meaning of green is the meaning of orange
and purple (and brown if yellow and blue mean
green and red). I suspect the brown of this table
can only be composed of blue and orange
and red and green and yellow and purple
(a brown of 3 blues, 3 yellows, 3 reds).
To remove any of these pairs will
"severely inhibit the rich texture."
The unavoidable meaning part may not
be what has impact. North is not up
unless the earth's the center of the universe
in thought as well as feeling.

If a green square is surrounded by
a pure yellow field, do we feel the blue
is what distinguishes it? Why isn't
a yellowish-green a bluish yellow?
Are we slumming it in form heaven?
Not if the paint's not dry and the difference
between lovers and friends who have sex
is the difference between green and yellow-blue
But just because it ain't easy bein' green
doesn't mean that it's any easier to be
one of the "primary elements" that flank it
unless of course dandelions and blueberries
are created simultaneously and leaves
an aftertaste like us.

Drinking Andy Warhol

What if America, teetering on the shell
The turtle hides in to see without having
To be with some Venus in burrs, stands solidly
On the fear there'll be more supply than demand?
Hence, Marketing. A Senator named after stage
Blood may be poured by his family onto the
Hamburger-shaped public arena to hide
Their selfishness in seeming sacrifice. Fame's
A stop on the way to health, but to loiter
In its lobby is to dwell upon a nipple
Forcing her to masturbate herself.
Indeed, somewhere the President's a Pawn
& he can't even tell me the difference
between Bold and Cheer.

I've heard the gaudy call of generic brands
& flatter myself as if nature dresses down for fear
Of being roped by cowpokes, raped by bulls in
The china shop knocking over the paper plates
That'd, otherwise, be as ignored as dollar bills
Viewed as leaves yellowed by inflation's piss
(Spring water in plastic bottles–that Penn & Teller
of the present) that many prefer to tap water.
How does the song go? "You don't see the earth complaining
About having to hurt somebody...You don't see the earth
Complaining/ You don't see what you're worth complaining..."

& What if the difference between heaven & hell is
A white dwarf & a red giant. The peach is Jupiter,
The cherry Mars. It's 3 AM & finally he's ready to
Kiss the sunset. The toilet clogged up, he'll shit
The secret into the park, modesty masquerading
As the fear of only being busted. Laws are needed to

Safely hate, yet walls are weeds and wants are needs
And sounds are getting to you, seducing you with "meaning."

Oh how you hate the authorities that go against
Your authority (the red light of conscience,
Both cop and whore, doing its best work under cover)
Because someone is simply there, wedging in between
What you see & what you do like a slap when a tickle
Will suffice to relieve you from the clothes that hide
Your skin (situations) from your eyes. What society wants
Is a detour from what it (when it's me) needs.
Ah! for a return to innocent selfishness!

But I must be developing a style
That tells you there's more to life than style
While we meet in the middle of an aisle
In a supermarket I am not going to be able
To get away shoplifting from if I stand here
Very loudly pretending it's an art gallery
To make a point about the price you pay
To make a point.

Advertising's aggressively defensive, but
There are times when "Order now, supplies
Are limited" or "Giddy up" can't give sanity
A leg to stand on like a soapbox. We're all
Retailers hightailing it into the trenches where
Demand meets supply like a businesswoman
& a punk trying to overcome their obvious differences
For the sake of a spark which hasn't yet ignited
The log which may be holding their dreamhouse up
Like a keystone or a crook. And when I'm bent
Into shape that they haven't noticed me lately,
I'm really just upset that I haven't noticed it lately.

Stealer's Wheel

1.
Because my mouth is watering
At the sight of the fountain I
Would only need to drink from
If my mouth weren't watering,
The heckler (got up as my heart)
Will only drink the water after
The juice has been poured
From a recyclable bottle
Into an unrecyclable carton
And just because he's hurt me
Doesn't mean he's malicious
Unless our carbon monoxide
Is more nourishing to the trees
Than the oxygen it was
Before we got a hold of it.

2.
You can't avoid what you can't control.
Even if it's not a blackout,
A candle won't envy a lava lamp.
Realities overlap like members
Of clubs being sued for their
    exclusivity
By someone who's not been
An outsider long enough
To not want to be in.
I like being here, but I won't
Be here tomorrow. If I like that
I will be here tomorrow
Unless you can be judged fairly enough
Without your actions being taken into account.

3
It's harder to live in reputation
Than in friendship so we call our
Professional relationships friendships
And our friendships love until love
Seems professional and whirling around
In the expediency of the moment where
All names are nipped in the bud, our
Prospects are not seen and so
Not seen as fair to middling
Until the giddiness of a quibble
Is found guilty of excessive wake up calls
Gripping the steel rail love pretends to be
When we're not in it so the smile
On the mask we call the void
Rubs off on all timid thieves who
Fall through it at the speed of lies
Even if music isn't a summer's day.

4.
"It can't be–Jesus would never
Come back as a golfer." But disbelief
Must eventually relent as life does
Unless I don't have to cut my bones out
To lose weight. "It's as if his mind
Pole vaulted out of his eyes."
Otherwise, I'll know only too well
That it can only exist if nothing else
Does. Why should I play a C chord
Once I learn a more difficult one?
Why should I turn my back on
Someone who left me to ratify a treaty
That puts a bandaid on the wound
That can't be healed anyway?

5.
My ex is no longer a judge and what
She calls my tendency to overanalyze
Is never as good as I hoped for nor
As bad as I feared so I'll be your patient
If you let me be your doctor. If not
I'll watch my four grandparents
Battle it out in me: In winter I'm
Alone and unhappy. In spring I'm
Alone but happy. In summer I'm
With people and happy. In fall
I'm with people and unhappy &
I wonder if sowing the seeds of thought
Will reap the harvest of emotion & how
Can the rich or tall have a headstart
If every second we start afresh?

6.
The wrong way of seeing things
Is still jealous of the right way.
I don't want sex–because to have sex
I have to call her. And I don't want
To be with her anymore (I mean right
Now). She knows this, but she's trying
To get me to think about sex to think
About her. If you could tax companies
Without them passing it on to workers,
Consumers, if she would cook and eat
For me, I'd have two less incentives
For wanting to cheat on her. And I need
Them to override the veto my libido
Threatens, but then backs down on.

7.
It's hard to keep my balance when love
Sits at the head of a round table.
If I had better eyes, you would have been
So naked when I first met you, I wouldn't
Have to worry about you leaving before
I forget you. I'm singing a song titled
"I must forget you (that's how I met you)"
& I'm not afraid you'll cheat on me with it
As long as I feel I have to be hurt to be
"In touch" with my emotions. Am I pouring
The grass cows eat onto the cereal you
Don't have to believe is breakfast to eat?
And how can I be the person I was when I
First met you without you leaving?

8.
When we first met, I knew we were
On rocking chairs. I don't remember
Whether we were rocking. Nor do I
remember if you had gray hairs
(though I remember loving them
if you did): "Did you hear about the
Old lady who crashed into Washington
Square, killing several..." I laugh.
"Sorry, I'm laughing..." "But what else
can you do?" "True, tears that heal
are scarce: Cry on this stump, it will
Become a leg. I wish." After awhile,
you said "I have to go. Nature calls."
"But Karla," I said, "Nature's always
Calling...it's just that it does so
Through different orifices."

9.
You had me in the sense that a driveway
Has a sidewalk. You had me the way a car
Has a lot of miles on it. You asked me
My sign. "Pisces." "Oh no, Pisces and
Aries aren't suppossed to get along!"
I guess that means I don't get along
With myself since I was born on the cusp.
You see me only as I am, not as I want to be
So I say you don't know me. But maybe
I see myself only as I want to be
So I whisper as the wind "As long as kids
Learn third person plural before first person singular,
at least I can rest assured you're not rejecting me."

10.
As long as kids continue to learn
Third person plural before first person singular,
Ripples move inward until the pebble
Is squeezed out from the surface of the lake
Like toothpaste from a tube.
But why does an arrow feel like the other arrow
It's aiming toward is really a target?
Probably for the same reason the fashion magazine
Says it's more of a cliche to think
In phrases than to think in words
(Though it does allow you to feel sorry
For the sexy unless you're sure they
Can't help it).

11.
A high pressure area the weathermen predicted
(But they're so rarely right I didn't
Plan my day around it), you must be
The girl of my dreams because every joke
I tell about anybody else fails to make me laugh
(Though granted a jest's prosperity lies
In the ear of those who hear it) and cry
and laugh about it all again. Yet I still
Must learn not to be disappointed when it
Takes me too long to realize your letter
Was a carbon copy addressed to the sun I'd be
If I could stand being clean shaven for
As much of the time as the percentage of
My body weight made from the water
That wouldn't pass the federal standards
That aren't enforced too much anyway.

12.
The feeling that I should like it more
May have led me to the heartbeat too steady
To be interesting unless juxtaposed with
The decorative complaints that side
With the flux against you. It's easier
To feel I'm writing to everyone when I'm
Writing to no one than it is when I write
To you. I only came here to be with you,
But I was ashamed of that because I hadn't
Spoken to you yet. So when you left,
I stayed here as if there was some other
Reason I came here and I bet there is.

13.
I walk through the crowds in pajamas
Because I'd rather be a suicide than a spectator
Because form is clever and content is passion.
I stand at the corner facing diagonally
So you'd think I was waiting for a redlight
(There's a second whe both are red, but
Never when both are green). In the photograph,
Someone who's only happy when outdoors is trying
To drive someone who's only happy in his house
Out of his mind. But the trees I can't see
For the forest are the times I'm not horny
Yet (stupidly) feel it's my duty to be
Until we all put our borrowed money
Where our borrowed mouths were.

14.
The silence I had to break
Because it wouldn't bend
Unless its poetic license had
Not expired but only exhaled
Was like a train that has to be filled
Beyond capacity to go slow enough
To have 20/20 vision and know
I'd be lying if I didn't tell you
I've just woken from a dream
In which a tooth I had pulled years ago
Came back as a dentist who
Wouldn't tell me about her past
As if I was made for horror and fear
Until horror and fear became you.

15.
But what if the difference between
Snow that blocks your view but never lays
And someone who flunked algebra because
He didn't show his work, though he got
All the right answers, is the difference
Between me and you? What if I couldn't
See you as a teacher until I needed to be
A student so much I'd get a scholarship?
Then we'll talk alot about becoming
Your opposite, of whether I like you
Or your place, of how "I don't want
To be like you at your age" means
"I want to be like you–but I can't
Do what you did to get there."

16.
I'll be listening to the words.
You'll be listening to the voice.
You'll be sitting. I'll be sitting.
I'll have to stand if I want to
Listen to the voice more than the words
But that doesn't mean that sitting for you
Is like standing for me. It must be time
To ask questions again, to start from
The scratch that scratches the skin off
So that the next time I feel so good
That the warehouse will be stocked
With answers, they won't have to
Lower their price unless it's not
As fun to put your finger on a thermometer
On a hot day as it is on a cold day.

When Depth Becomes Vice
for Ange Mlinko

I woofed down the present, the whole contemporary era,
spent the last dollars of my last paycheck
the exact second I got this one (and what kind of heaven
is that?) just so you couldn't get under my skin
like a debt to finger what I fall back on,
the money-like memories saved for the rainy day (of death)
in which the seeds which took so long to be seen
as fledgling shoots grow from less than an inch high
to ten feet tall while my back is turned for only a second
I swear and what kind of heaven is that?

Then my respect for you grows like a new wing
of a hospital that'll never get off the ground
because you rejected the way I was it seems aoens
ago, the surface not the depth, but would only hold
a grudge if it could hold water like a person who has
to be a name or fate in order not to be a disguise, a corpse.

So if it's okay not to ration, there was no way (in hell)
I could have been doing nothing but scraping out
the little bit of jelly left in the bottom of the jar
onto the unmultipliable bread I can't live by alone
even if crust or toast: the firm bread of my
soggy history, the scoreboard of I I keep on
the backburner you block my view of
and it's only inside me if you are too
since it's only inside me if it's outside me
which doesn't mean I'm gonna give back the money
or that it's raining so much I don't have to be hungry

18 1/2 Minute Gap

If there wasn't this interference,
I could make myself perfectly clear
and the one who wants such clarity
would certainly be happy
if statues could be happy
and maybe they can [laughter]
because each one of us has to
identify with a statue sometimes
(or else there'd be no couples)
and even the lowliest among us
(I say, as if with all the authority
of experience behind me)
have to be happy sometimes
and who's to say it isn't
the statue part of us which feels such joy?
Well, me, but I too am another statue
(of a pigeon that shits on a statue)
and am only part of you if the sky is,
and it is, it is, and speculation
is this interference. But it's also saturday.
Listen, children, all is not lost
and clear interference reminds me
that one can be drunk on soberness
and yesterday's desperate desire
to be simple again is, no doubt,
around here somewhere,
even if I am a crook.

Over and Over

If I thought I could tell you my first thought
Was that there's something other than thought
Without fearing I was lying, we could make love
On the first night without feeling like we're
Missing out on anything. If there were no sex
Before marriage, we'd be married before we're born.

If I didn't have hands, the plane would never
Touch down. I wouldn't be everybody because
I wouldn't be anybody & I wouldn't have pockets
Unless they had holes in them. You wouldn't
Have a mouth if I didn't have ears & I wouldn't
Have ears if I didn't have hands that wanted
To hang limp while I wanted to touch you.

A wind wouldn't touch you if it didn't wear gloves
That are the men who cheat on me with you because
They're part of me unless the plane runs out
Of fuel over the ocean I love as a runway shattering
The statue I'd be if I didn't have hands to hold me
So I can hold you when you're literally alone
With me, especially if we lie about it.

100% Beside Myself

I don't have to fight to see your brown eyes
but neither do I have the right to see your brown eyes.
I may, however, have to fight with myself
for thinking I have the right to see your brown eyes.

I do not deserve you, but I don't believe anybody
deserves anybody. So I am not insecure & not alone.
I am alone, but at least I know that I'm not alone
in being alone. Does this mean I'd feel more alone
when I'm with people, for instance, you?

I wouldn't rule it out, but then I have a hard
time ruling anything out. Not always, of course.
Now, for instance, I'm doing a pretty good job
of ruling out whatever it is that doesn't want
to see you tomorrow night, whatever it is
that doesn't want you to be over your sickness.

Actually, the desire to see you sick
didn't even occur to me until now,
and seeing that I'm in a purely decorative mood,
I wouldn't worry about it if I were you

but if you did, I wouldn't worry about
your worrying if I were me, which I may
not be (unless you rule that out
so we can love the wall less travelled).

The Shape I'm In

"As long as I don't have someone to know,
I have no one to know but my self,
The self as a medium through which I know
Not others but life in the form of relatons
Between self and others, others and others,
Self and self, self as relation..." Oh mercy.

You must be merciful to ask for mercy.
You cannot be merciful unless you ask for mercy.
This loveless shiver has been with me
A home away from home on a day
That wouldn't seem average at bottom
Were it not disguised as hell and highwater
Where you have to say hello to the cop
To wish happy birthday to the horse beneath it
Turning a corner now, out of sight and soon mind
As I play music to watch grrrls-even-if-they're-with-guys-by
On my laptop keyboard (but that's just my leash on life).

One turns her back and smiles as I do a little flourish
At the end of the bridge to "The Shape I'm In."
This, and the wind blowing her long black dress up
Just enough to advertise her yellow boots,
Nudges light through the shadow of the leaves
A breeze bids dance on my notebook to the sound
Of boots and engines and though this comes
Too near the praising of myself the mere sight
Of an unhelmeted cyclist reminds me there are
Birds nearby, not yet usurped.

Reparations, Preparations

Why sing of alluminum shadows
when your perception of me is surely
that of an ice cream bullet
if precisely you could see
by means of pain outside the theatre,
in its shadow, dying to get out
and hog the podium or lick the skin
lingering lazily above the semi-closed lips
of a kiss ungratefully received
now that the sugary tarmac
of short term memory is revealed
to be the moon covered by clouds
under stealth of night
and blue is doubly distanced
like singing the blues to rid you of them
but violence breeds violence
and (eagerness picks up the pace)
sex is violence and lady sings the blues
better than the tramp that gives
a little bit of its life for you
and only women bleed
and men always come
and certain bad jokes are
more beautiful than others
and I can create the fashion
and get you in the ward
where I am the doctor and not the fish
because nothing is fishy but the flame
and no one's a loophole but the loop
in the slideshow where everyone's a star
and you don't have to die before you live
and here's a place in the country everyone's ideal
and here's a couple of kooks hung up on romancin'
and here's my last duchess and next up is The Jam

with "The Butterfly Collector" and if I say
you don't have to know what it refers to
but suspect that you do know
I am perhaps mildly chiding you for playing,
for reading, when it would be far more useful
to chide others for going to too many
chucklefests they call poetry readings
but at least I know the contours of
the many small Greek God figurines
that bubble up from time to time
in the melting pot to greet the TV eye
she's got on me and soon she will be you,
the quicker picker upper, my favorite mutinee
and there's a certain thrill that isn't gone
as the moon behind memory is another memory
and I see it when I'm in the bathroom
on the east side where, brushing my teeth
with beauty, I catch myself identifying
with Ebenezer realizing it's earlier than he thought
as well as Jackson singing "it's later than it seems"
and I need to put them in a room together
without it turning into John Ritter
unless it also turns to "Reach Out In The Darkness"
and Cameo singing "Word Up" with a side of Syd
and scrubbing bubbles that do not accuse me
of losing the opportunity of exhibiting
a moral lesson when I supress the dialogue
between the usurper and the hermit
because they know damn well the rebirth
of wonder sick of waiting because I'm
very colorful with Gena and Ethel tomorrow
even if you don't show up on my birthday
and that this (and the way you wear
the Manhattan Bridge, and thus the D,
the Q and the B, low on the hip) is part
of your charm and therefore part of mine
and it's okay that we're prudes
and they're still fucking peasants as far as I see.

We Cancel Each Other Out in Prose
for Liz Brennan

1.
What the explicators couldn't erode
Promised permanence in all forms but prose
If I crack the coldness of its code
If I expose it's all a pose
I wonder if it would look good in my clothes.

2.
An essay attacking makeup is the pot calling the kettle black. You can't be a wild philosopher unless you're a competent tailor for Butcher & Singer. The fear that the infinity that sucked us in was just the snazzy packaging for a mundanity demanding total commit- ment and a loss of that renaissance man freedom we abused as an adolescent but would surely treat better now if only we could climb a Himilayan peak with sofas on our backs...

3.
Even though "it's your moral obligation to act out of self-interest" sounds suspiciously like "Make 'Em Speak English," it's better than trying to explain the earth without taking the sun into account. Praise and blame gang up on indifference in vain. The dog of checks and balances has had its day. A word is bothered by meaning and a man reduced by words feels worse than a man reduced to words. A system falls apart and rebuilds itself faster than another one that condemns it as a mere slogan. But what can you do when the anti-graffiti league is hot on your track & you gotta let something out?

4.
There can be no system that doesn't take into account the fact that there can be no system. The feeling of moral superiority may have gotten you through winter, but spring comes like the feeling that

ridiculousness has its advantages over being too careful, as if "If I'm too sloppy, you're not sloppy enough" is just my way of saying "I'm Okay, You're Okay" and the only way to stop seeing yourself as a kid is to have one.

5.
The folks who make up stories of anthills ruined by rain to claim that ants aren't conscious (so we can be conscious for them) have made the distinction between saying and doing a necessity. It created more jobs which were supposed to signify revitilization until G-d slammed shut the door of the Red Sea in the face of the Pharoah's Army of explanatory prose that lagged behind the it I'm sometimes grateful you mistake for me, as long as getting tangled in the web of idolatry is the only thing that saves you from the solipsism which perpetuates society in the form of groupies who falsely feel they could flunk the sobriety line-walking test if they really tried, as if there's a choice of desserts marketed as main courses to the stomach if not the tastebuds.

6.
Every time my body calls me away from my self, I stop writing (and everytime I stop writing my body calls me away from my self). But how do you define the fear of the half-hearted ocassonalist? Is the only marriage that can be made in heaven the marriage of heaven and hell? Can you embrace uncertainty and still resist wishy-washiness? Such obsessive questions are brought to you courtesy of that which prides itself on thinking it's redefining the boundaries of poetry. But if that's all it's doing, it might as well say "Hey babe they're playing our song" only when the National Anthem comes on.

7.
One could complain that only poets read poetry or rejoice that everyone who reads poetry is a poet. That advances in the art of neglecting basic needs may have led some here, but to complain on their behalf is like punching out an income tax form I swear! Does it really matter if I'm out to attack falsity more than to generate truth? So what if I

wish to crowd the void with the junk that satirizes how you crowd the void with junk? I'm not trying to absolve myself; I'm just trying to get you to stop absolving yourself. The only reason truth can't sarcastically be expressed is because it can't be expressed. I only like the sarcastically embodied truth for its body. Ah, to be a superfluous part of the lowest common denominator I wouldn't envy were it not too late to be past danger!

8.
Somehow the end-in-itself snuck through customs, dodged the checkout counter. Maybe we should hire store detectives to wait between stations, wear our Sunday best only on Tuesday afternoons until they become corrupted by explanations and expectations as silly as weather mistaken for winter to one who lives in the country disguised as the city where means to an end windowshop for philosophies too fat for love in the form of a couple to swallow.

9.
I start seeing solitude as the trial that's just about to begin (after a lengthy jury selection which, of course, wasn't substantial) when my roommate comes back with his girlfriend to watch The Simpsons. If I really care about these silent moments I must defend them. But I let them go, because they weren't "treating me well." Accusing a mirror of domestic violence, blaming the tea I didn't leave on the burner long enough for being cold. Not that it cares if I blame it (or maybe it does and that's the point).

Coda.
It went on like this for years then mortality convinced me once again in a flash that the urge for reason and order shouldn't be allowed to be dressed up with no place to go, that I might as well show it the town (of tenderness mistranslated as transcendence), or let it show me the town, which I could never see with its eyes, though I may look cute in the glasses it gave me (but only to it who now was blind).

III

Lingua Franca

If only now you were to emerge from
the shelter of the bell whose clapper
has been using you as a punching bag,
the hurt which merges with the headlines,
as long as we're content to listen
in every form but speech,
would be the leaves that wouldn't
have fallen had you not gotten
such a kick out of shaking the tree.

Emerge for faith's ready with cameras
to shoot commodities of comfort
as long as love is valued
before forgetfulness is accepted
as an ocean that holds its own
as well as a bumpersticker
which keeps togetherness content
enough to sleep beneath the clouds
that cover the stars like reporters.

Emerge and let them fall from
the isolation which is not solitude
and which haunts all but the
naughtiest of the hungry on
the ship of life we watch go down
from the rafts that would be a shore
if you could be an island without
harbouring lush vegetation
which is only frutiful to spill
over the sides, unmuzzle and multiply
to bring them to the knowledge
that loaves and fish would not nourish
were they not also pain and poison.
But don't expect them to

pardon our French in a land
where the English they make us speak
sees swearing as obscene and forgets
the tightrope walker needs no net
for the same reason a net doesn't.

Three Poems for Laura Moriarty

1. Snorting Up the Pound-Williams Line

Some selves are fluttering kites
You can't see without strings attached
Unless they're tangled in a tree
You'd cut down were it not
For the fruit it bears known to cause
The indigestion without which I fear
The tree would fly into the final fronteir
Like the table even laying all my cards on
Won't prevent from rocketing
Unless you sit on it soon. It may be crushed
If you sit on it too soon, though there's
Little danger of that this time of night.

2. Leaping Before We Look

Passion is a stick figure. I know
not what I say and saying
is doing and whispering needs
to pull the rug of the race
out from under the caboose
of the train that wouldn't be
thought were not its tracks
the pain the judge pretends
to throw out of court like the prayer
the defendant starts thinking he has
in a bottomless pit that has been
known to be clean as a whistle
until we stop blowing on it, tame
as a thimble until we try to tame it

3. As a Penny Runs from Money

To the extent the hero is a braggart
and victory at best a welcome mat
to a house I can no longer fill with thoughts
of you without faith in pointlessness
and the coin of defeat that's flipped
so many times it seems to be melted down
when life is a furnace only to those who
can walk through the fire they didn't
know was a flatterer until it cried
"long live the log" to reveal the trees
who've just slipped out of the leaves
but haven't slipped into snow
and the sun no longer blocked
for the same reason it no longer warms.

Sirhan Sirhan

Solitude has begun to burn the log of self
but the two have not become the unity
of which ash is the visible half-truth.
Foolish ash, who prides yourself
on being the only child of the marriage
of log and flame. You can only
sing through sisters of air. But dualism
denies debate. Log turns ash. Flame becomes air.
No connection but immaculate conception.
Foolish ash of the unassailable future
Disguising yourself as a log
to "protect" the trees presenting solitude
as a forest fire which means less to the forest
than the wooden houses not yet built–
as if one can see without eyes
or that all that one can see is eyes.
Surely they're mine. Everything is.
Surely pain is an illusion,
and the loss which makes a tree ash
without becoming a log
may warm those by the fireplace
in the summer house of the sun
in which we live and die each second
eluding the censors for sure
and eluding the senses we redefine
as body tingles a word like mind.

Rain Parade

1.
Desire is only a drug when distant from
the love returned to as obsession or duty–
obsessionally shuttling
between obsession and duty
as if truth and beauty are
goalposts and you a football
oblivious to how many times
you've changed hands.
This, too, has the kind of benefits
we've been warned against
by spokesmen of desire
so defensive they point
everything toward a target
that is only a woman if Venus
is more of a woman than
the foam she rises from.

2.
No means maybe maybe yes.
But yes means yes. There is
An asymmetry in Venus born of foam.
The need to feel at fault for
Something an other may have
Enjoyed well enough names guilt
The god of gravity. Your duty is
To keep your mind on the immanence
you fear most (and your immanence
is to keep its mind on the duty you fear most)
provided you're not too busy fearing fear
in which thoughts of relationships
rain on the parade of the present
and what tells you "you shouldn't feel pain"
is not discredited once you realize it is
the pain it warns you against
and you're in so deep you act humble
the better to eat them with
(though they won't tell you
where they put your teeth).

Now that It's April and January Is Back in America

The motion of a myth mattering more
Than the myth of motion, mattering
More than matter. To make matter matter...
To take the name of brain and shove it,
Shove off. The ship of state, what sinks
When every particle waves–

We don't have to OD on the solitude
We begrudge, though the relationship
The urge for comparisonsn has with feelings
Of regret seems to last forever. Plus
The popping of the balloon is the desire
To abandon ship, to miss the boat by
Calling one's boat the sea. Allegedly,
"La Bamba" means "I am not a sailor,
I am a captain, I am a captain." And then
We get to the king of kings thing
As we pass another burger
Oh we should treat ourselves better!
The stanza that never ends.

So many threads to pick up. Enough
Ivy climbing the walls to ignore,
To invoke the draft we feel to forget.
Does anybody remember to feel? Has
anybody seen my love? I don't care
What I care about until responsibility
Seems to be a drab way of putting what
Grounds me if remembering has everything
To do with identity and love loses
No more than it gains in the personification
Like a hot windy day that can happen everyday
Even without the fixed boundaries
That fool us into what uncomfortably

Passes for mutuality, but based in fear,
Faithless fear, not without good reason
And our own house dressing
A selling point for what may be freer
In less capital-intensive solitude
Unless we get a kick admitting
We love to see life as nothing but money
Shots that seem to get harder to find
And so we try to stand on the prophetic point
Like it's the end, having got further into
The light an we're accustomed, as if it's
Early spring & we think we can leave
More than winter behind.

Things To Do with Fire

I live by myself from a fire,
I live from myself by a fire.
I am subtracted from a fire
and who doesn't matter so much
as what (the fire said, the shadow of fire)
comes between. Death by fire, bodies crackling,
smoke so we don't see the other side, never.

I've seen enough of fire
but one can't turn one's back on death
without turning her back on life.
So sleep, it comes in sleep.
Wake up, the coffee, quick,
before dreams come disguised
as memories of sleep, the other side,
the chicken that crosses to get
lives in time while the egg that rolls
for the feeling of crossing lives in sleep.

To walk through flames and not get burned
by the fear, to be distinct just to
be extreme. The fear of fire becomes a fire
I walked through once, my 'wants' intact,
complaining about the darkness, the alien,
the undestroyed destroyer my actions
slept with behind my back.

If the fire writres this, the fire reads this.
On the edges, might as well be water,
might as well as water, lazy lighthouses
sending smokesignals to each other
flattered by their fear! We live by what
we die to do. But the fire can be calm as seems.

The silence, the patience of fire
(whose dream we are). It only seems to rage
as our pillowtalk of origins is thunder to
the heroic cockroach of song. Yet we live
in such seeming, the feeling of fire become word,
the tyranny of mimetic denotation subverted
by aesthetic connotation. Self-generating,
shameless exhibition until a word douses
the flame by looking at it, the lost core
of loss, molten, molthing, in its way, its prey.

Things To Do After All Hell's Broken Lose

You wanted to talk. But even if it's just a toy bomb you
dropped on the dollhouse it still takes awhile to pick up
the pieces and even with remote control changing channels
can be a strain and by the time I do it (but before
the apllause has set in) the static cuts you off.

Distance can evaporate in the box of writing
& that's scary as if the body (disguised as sex) is
the Isaac Abraham is told to toss or else.
But every judge is a defendant & a triangle falls
into the sludge & the mathematic system of marriage
may have to be erased so we can see
the sky as other than a roof of fear
to build our own rood so we have something that could fall...

I will not blame you for getting under my skin
and I will not take your confusion personally.
I will take it personally, but not as an affront.
Have faith, be patient. Don't be a dupe for a dream.
A war between "don't think about it" and
cathartic "mimesis." It is the longest day of the year.
Oh, it has such societal significance.
Sighs do, thighs do. Trust and lust.
Oh math, are we equals? Oh physics, do we fit?
And doubt, just what are you driving at
if not economics?

In the flotation tank it hits me how cold
and cruel I lapsed into the justice game like suits
one could start "wanting" to wear all the time.
The way I've been with others (and solitude)
provides no blueprint, but fearing the thorn
at comes with the rose doesn't soften
the thorn that's here without it.

For M.

I am so in love with a moment
I may call my self today if
I got nothing to do but the mirror
in whom I only music the meanings
in the glamourous black I build so I notice
the stick of lightning you slid in the slot
and see you as the money
your mere presence can sheathe
as we'll cast ourselves in festival terms
though the haze doesn't clear
the celestial speedtrap for which
the walls of sex have no ears
as you find yourself checking to see
if it's a sonnet if the passion
through which actions gaze at polemics
like these can shatter the mood of a name
as meanings and music meet in the melting pot
clutching each other more fiercely than
you and I do in the jalopy of memory
(where the undercover cop searches
for hitchikers, makes what s/he finds
and though we must resist it in love
we cannot do so without being its dupe).

The Verdict

I pray to be rid of a passing pomposity
to make way for a more permanent presumption
from the wound we would give ourselves
to fill the one we gave each other
when the desire to control silently fights
the desire to know–
the absolute zero of garden variety ghosts....
the universe a snubbing thumb!
The past lies dead, as if distorted, a photo
in a scrapbook memory revises in a darkroom
not unlike the cover under which we fucked
if foreplay can be considered fucking
for when we'd throw the covers away
as if nakedness if nothing but orgasm
memories are so many there seems to be none
and before they fade there may yet be
a supernova as if it's not September
but early April in July
so we do unto others what experience
does to the meanings of words once sugared
on hilltops, steeples and billboards
to spread a blanket for the dawn
that promises nothing for solitude
but time's broad brushstrokes
presumptuous as a mouth we put words in

until the mouth becomes a word
not oblivious to the throw away society
ineluctable even to losers in their loud laments
read as a luscious secret by young rebels
or misfits (the verdict's not in) en route
to a more fleshed out articulation
of pain and what it pretends to prevent
as if a painter so drunk on possibility

he can no longer renounce realism
with a straight face in the clouds
without admitting the deformity
whose shallowness has discovered
what eluded all our wisdoms.

My Daughter Would Be a Novelist

The invisible hand that fingers each authentic witness
is amputated by a cruelty necessary as a corrective as long as
skepticism is virile, akin to the wind teasing the air.
Oh conventions, why hast thou let me forsake thee!
Aren't these, too, conventions?
Philosophers, be as your words.
Thing-in-itself, fly east and meet the id on top
of the empire state on v-d day in a marriage
by violins that eke out pouts because mercenaries know
the score by score, know the muse of muzak
awaiting us all like a pop fly one could
see as a CEO if one is inclined, inflated
a balloon that cannot feel without popping
the places I picture myself in:
the scenes I make in order to have something to be behind,
the museums that prop up the money and give it
the excuse it needs so the sun can shine
were there not folks with skin cancer
who can only identify with moments of joy
by being a traitor to a government
that should not be destroyed until it's built.
We kid ourselves to believe it governs us.
In fact, we've never had parents.
Definition eludes us like rage
that will return to scold itself
for scolding us unless we can can
new pleasures in the sun of ceremony,
dumb but happy, made of money
and therefore poor as paper
beneath the surface of beauty
where the slamdance of connotations
holds its own and suspicion is suprisingly serene.

Allowance Money that Is Death to You

Miracles are molecules only microscopes get sick of.
Loneliness is the freedom to be caught smiling
By a machine you have to kick a pigeon off to ride.
A gavel bangs and its echo is intercepted
By the cushioning of a faith while I play
The flipside to "Love The One You're With"
As if it were the enemy of love that evaporates
When you forget yourself in a sheet of sound
To numb the screams of promises we made
To pretend to put the breaking point on hold
For as long as it takes to ride west with someone
I have to catch myself to be jealous of
For purely dramatic reasons.

I hold my tongue until sanity goes on strike
And stinks up the place with saints
That threaten to dub you satan until vexed
By breathing past the treelines of martyrdom
Into the silence that's really the next poem
Unless you can stir the clouds out without the coffee
Raining up into your face on a swing casting shadows
On the stars that treat me to all kinds of strategies
With no place to go but the house that has
So many mansions no Bible can hold it
Without being burned like the butcher cover
I blow when colder than cash until cleverness
Becomes crescive en route to a storm
Between the lines of a joke that goes over
Too well in Arkansas to ever succeed from the ear.

Hope for the Wicked

Is like hell for the heavenbound, a threat
of piety polluting what otherwise would
endlessly earn the name of comfortable freedom
that doesn't need to be fleshed out but slips
in an out like what corpses call a ghost
like what men and fish call a frog...
to itself no hybrid, music and meaning, the mistletoe
of estrangement, all the fucking flags flooring those
who thought the war was over.

But perhaps there is no way out–
just because you know what comes up must go down
doesn't mean the man with the house on his head
doesn't have to worry about plumbing
when the go between proves harder to seduce
and the bridge didn't take the flood into account
and the message gets tangled in the messenger.

You're invited, almost commanded, to blame
the ideals even the body can become
and position yourself upon
the dotted line of seemingly antiseptic doubt.
It harbors passion, but must seem as dull and cold as stone,
to itself at least if not to those who pretend to sing
strictly from an alien perspective and who
may yet receive compensation
for finding their temper by losing it
and screaming their ambitions
as if the ambulance rushing to heal the dead
has not run over the living in the process
that is hope and life's abundance,
safer than average, a complex gong.
I am destroyed. Let them fuck with me.

Fish Story

The things we see our reflections in
have no time to reflect and are not things.
A reflection is seen. Of what? Not me
until I comb my toupe, am thrown for
a loop I can only see when still.
I am never still, but my shed skins are.
I put on a snakeskin suit
and leave the driving to them. It's cute
to be lead around by the dead.
I must be a deadhead. But even the dead
die and I refuse to go phishing
and so become fish. It is my sign.
Better to be a big fish in a shrinking pond
than those with rods and hooks.
I cann no longer eat and must be eaten.
The drought makes me an easy catch.
As the hooks sent from the boats sink in,
I notice the fishers too busy seeing their reflection
in what's left of the water to look me in the eyes.
Well, you might as well cook me.
But after being photographed alongside of me,
you throw me back. Afraid of what I'd do
inside of you?

IV

Flattened Until Dishevelled

1.
He who held you up is holed up until hooted off
by those who anticipate the end beyond the end
and circle round everything like the nothing we are
between names. All you ever wanted was an hour
of noon, a state of revolt, just shy of a box lunch.
But these laser maniacs of welcome wave us on
toward a glass of doctor's belongings, lost repairs,
the too many choices found in the hermits'
abandoned submarine of laughter gone stale
til a leak is sprung like an antique in a newsflash
of verse to enpurple the already blue alimentary
media res through jungles tortured and ticklish
and saluting those who seem to refuse the saliva
cones of generosity's downsized hotplate in a
long blackout coat that makes winter superfluous
as a quarterback's sneeze, a salesman's squeeze

2.
Then solitude becomes the shower to absorb
the sweat my fans I mean friends can not–
as serious as the spontaneity of a smile
made secret by the season it is powerless
to not signify. If the proud molecule of summer
demands a tomb against its fickle offspring,
as a fallout shelter gives birth to bombs of applause
and the absence of any small change without blowhorns
where leaves might as well be cement to the sun's
masturbatory whining intimacy in which knowledge
is useless as odorless gastanks until labour wanes
like what laziness, aloof, calls love without lovers
hijacked by skeptics they must become as
the footprints of the invisible hand are followed.

3.
The similes that are happening to me now
help the theatre parachute from the plane of risk
where reality gets laid by the smoke in search of
a fire of confused advantage. And one falls
to the familiar with the assistance of a coat of pain,
a monument one drapes over the mudpuddle
for the sake of an obsolete lady in a world gone thrillers
whose exaggerations rob desire of all but
the premature tenderness of a cabbage head
rolling on the cement outside the stranded theatre
and back on the plane whose pilots own no cars
but the chalk that wouldn't make me sneeze
were it not bored with the board it resembles
if the sky is too shy to let you shine in it.

4. (Between Tests)
The prices, like defenses drop.
The emotions that were your identity consume themselves
brining water to labour from nature at last
as the question of home ownership becomes
an arsonist's empire and time is ice.
Here in the hills, we made love in the
form of a hike that wouldn't be fooled
by the clothes you were among.
The assignments we awaited like party poopers
and the sun that makes paltry paupers of "us all"
while time hides in the lengthening shadows
death casts when it sticks its neck out
in dreams of shelter children remind us of
until we make them wash up in the middle
of the cartoon to bring them cruelly
to indifference even if it means nothing
but a shiver down your spine with a self up its sleeve

Fragile Blonde

My self-reliant vertebrae of light
is too missing in action to be a prisoner of war.
It knows no shame, is had by no name
though they, like suitors, use it as a mirror
to impress themselves with their despair
and the triumph of pain over potbellied despair
where pain becomes pleasure in the apocrypha
that streaks by, skinny, like the black bird
with orange wings we swear we saw on the bridge
from which more nameable sparrows were seen
to bathe in the furious reflection of our curious smiles
with no sighs to prop up the baggage of drought
that circles around the corpse like non-pejorative parasites
striking the set of the coffin by making it cry
in public like a traffic jam on a day so beautiful
sacrifice is unavoidable. Each self, even the ones
called sexist, must flourish in the concrete jungle
of collage that's getting too big for its unisex breeches
where everything's a mask but immortal abstractions
that can not be staged without sensurround, whispers,
burps and questions created equal to the task and trough
as if each second is a sabbath kept holy by holes I am
until you halo me in a catalogue that contains us only be becoming
unglued in a prelude which swells the banks of the song
I'm pretending to be commisioned to write all night
by a constancy who wants to see me small, ground me
against a wall to shuffle the deck of ceremony out of fear the dreck
I escaped by the scruff of a neck, alone, in tennis,
whose nerves would have me so kept and pointless
in peacetime until the suitor dressed up with no
place to go, the clothes blowing from the line,
demand I shoplift them and, mutually empowered,
we are imprisoned in a sitcom, singing remakes
of the simplicity signed on the dotted line of

seen-through hooplah, though secret to those
who have a stake in the snake conventions,
the smoke filled rooms of the garden party
about to be fired, in anticipation of that sacred moment
that bosses us around if we're willing.

Professions of Faith

Community may be a bridge from one to another
and the bridge may serve no function.
The water might as well be dry when swimming is walking
and part of me is further away from me
than you will ever be (except in thought,
the disenchantment which is not detachment).
To see a queen in every pawn, to love the mediators
more than the goal may be unnecessary entanglement,
a waste of time and breath. Go ahead, betray your
half-assed desire for what can't happen later
if it doesn't happen now. If now were the time for
clandestine meetings under cover of death, sensuality
would smother the love that's nothing to it, the love
that cannot care what I, or any body, thinks of it;
a jar in Tennessee that could be taken for
a new born babe with wild wolves all around it.

I go on peaceably, in a kind of defiance
with a stick up my butt. No, that's the figure
in the painting I can only see my reflection in
when blotting and being blotted before the paint dries.
The paint never dries. This is the history of the present
divvied up among a couple quarreling in doggeral
about the fate of their daughter who becomes the freedom
of the sun enforcing the norms of a subculture
I'm proud to claim as present when I take my place
at the podium just to get your goat. You see, we're
already hooked; try as I might to wriggle out
from under the burden of immortality.
It's no boast to say in words that all is words.
Yet equivocation must spare at least the value of
friendship. I had to go very far into the slums of
vagueness and reputation to drown out the voices
of the dead I thought were living threats.

The decorative pursued me like a harness and
even to recount it is to count on it as a kind of crutch
that's kindling for the fire of the present that is the community
in which an atom is always split in two
in order for some me to get to some you.

An Infantilization of Infinity

The pie that shrinks when more people
want a piece of it is false. "I can't even
tell the difference between artificially
flavored cherry & strawberry and you
expect me to be ethically subtle." What's
wrong with this picture if war's looking
it straight in the eyebrow?

I search the warehouse of strategies.
All I see is ruins. There must have
been a warehouse once. The testimony
of others assures me. They're not
ruins, they're virgin rocks. You have
to be in a hole this thick, like an
amputee trying to live hand
to mouth, to notice them. At least I did.

You can't fool father culture unless you're
mother nature and most decidedly I'm not
so let's get tangled in the attempt to avoid
entanglements. At least until the reinforcements
arrive. The ones that someone tries to blame me
for not being on time, as if I'd stoop to such a thing.
The nerve! After all I've done, kept it under my wing,
catering to its every need, which I, of course,
know better than it does. How wrong I've been.
I repent. Let's go to a mall, a movie, ask for
donations, as if we're on the sunny side of
the difference between a physical and a
psychological addiction, as if the icing is
easier to get rid of than the cake you let
go to pot like some defense departments,
er, democracies, we know.

If there's a tightrope walker, we're the
net that really wants to catch her. We get
thrown out of court during earthquakes (and
the earth only comes in the form of quakes).
Those were the seconds, my sloppy friends.
You're not really yelling at yourself in the
second person and politics makes a good salad
on a holiday by a woodstove in sweaters of
joy falsely attributed to the kind of storybook
success that happens more to the reader than
the characters the author must become in
the process in order not to go chasing after
some past that happens in the headlines of
the papers you only read for the want ads.

Law of Diminishing Returns
for Bernadette Mayer

A rocket scientist is afraid of being tied
to the escape route. The thermostat
taxpayers insist is thermometer
shoots through the ozone hole to announce
which way the spring (too busy making up
for last winter to be itself) wavers
like a senator, a shoehorn gathering dust
in an age of rollerblades.

The word revolution caught sleeping
on the job is punished by being promoted.
It is not anger in the hope culture is
more of a window onto nature than a wall,
Nor desire in the moonlight of
the yin-yang logo whose eyeglasses
it's better to force the blind to wear
than never invent. But fear is the eye
that cannot open without being the wound
that doesn't get a return on its investment.

We thought we measured but merely made
that which we tried to sell in Pepsi cups
that had this nasty habit of turning into Grecian Urns
though without the precision only achieved
by a moment which is not transcendence
but what tenderness would be were passion
believed in as easily as maxims turn ghosts
and ghosts professionalized so the theatregoer
(who won't make a bearable actor until it's
a playwright) continues to be a slave to a plot
that promises to be less linear when it grows up
(which should happen every time now).

For Kurt Cobain

And though death may have less to do
with what's gone AWOL from a name
than the American quest for a final frontier
leaving the cities, where I live as an outcast
filthier than ruins but in spring when I write
what I couldn't take on face value
without feeling pinned down not so much
by the materialist as by the biographer's
mundane parody of memory
not mutable enough to isolate a mood
incapable of the adoration
of the connoisseurs whose rectangles
taboo their flowers which taboo our weeds
and never put themselves on trial

just to raise issues like children
who yell at us by being themselves
to look at clouds from the plane
that cannot complain because it should
and, led on by the desire to get it out
of our system, we 'settled' for having gotten
it out in public called private by those
who only matter, who aren't as 'bugged'
by the suburbs as much as by the ego
(unles the suburbs take the form of ego)
and the evil of those who die young
remains unsanctified but as entertainment
taken straight as the path of least resistance
with no chaser but the tail-chasing Romanticism
seems like to the mannikins who wouldn't do
the ostrich to meet the sand halfway
though it only makes housecalls on the plane
that can't complain about duty admitted
as a formal concern to vindicate the narcissism

an ex-President would dub it
on the well policed playgrounds of the mind
where no kids bite past 12
but those who spit the song out
to sell them all for food
now that the flags are halfmast
to prove he was a crook

Partly Claudia

1.
Partly me. The calculations: She tries to figure out
why he's trying to figure her out. When people
try to figure each other out it's surely love.
When lovers try to figure each other out it's
surely doomed. A shoot sprouts in time for
the first frost. The dollar you gave me that
may have meant more had you been poor
is seen scorning the god of shivers I nervously
bow down before. If sex is everywhere I
better admit I'm to blame for being tired
(as a loophole for the sake of the space I'm
no good for you without).

2.
The passions that return when the distance
I have on the agony of lust is a house of cards
in a teapot I can't see for the tempest.
I love you but where there's smoke (uncertainty)
there must be fire (faith) and if not in you
in something ("Better a hermit with no friends
than a socialite with falsies.") So I swim
in shark infested waters as if I too am shark,
or water. Hatred rises from the dross, the gloss
for one lousy honest minute. Then shame cloaks
it in irony as if *that's* closer to love.

3.
If healthfood can only be healthy if it's eaten
everyday, how can I make this sweet without
Making us fat? And where's the prologue
to remind "the ladies" the lion is but snug

the joiner when the conversation only gets
going after the 3rd or 4th goodbye stops to
see if death has taken off the clothes of its
checkered flag connotations because I've
overgeneralized from the few times its interests
and "the earth's" united against a common enemy?
It's hard to imagine falling in love without
having first fallen in love with love so I play
sick so you can play Doctor by refusing to play
any God but the one whose religion I gave up for lent.

4.
We made love in the hospital bed,
posed downtown policemen for our scrapbook,
watched democrats leave in droves (a bad sign
for republicans). The question of jealousy
never came up, and when it did, it was only
to applaud us for keeping our cool. What Freud
would have to say about it is more boring
than what you would. You could say anything,
as long as it's you. You you you. "If you'll
be my shelter I'll be your storm," said the fly
to the flame, spider to the mouth, kiss to
the curse. Now I sit in the sunlamp of the sun.
Memories cast off their clothes of promise.
We meet through the backdoor, our 'fixed'
address hard to make out. "Sneakin' Sally
Through The Alley" sounds a little more soulless
each day. Days turn into years; nostalgic
for nostalgia. It's the first thing they teach us,
even before we have anything to be nostalgic for.
But what they didn't tell us was that adulthood
is little more than wearing things out
before we outgrow them.

5.
I thought I loved you as a tiger loves his cage
(turns out I loved you as a person loves a picture
of a tiger in a cage). Police protection passed
for lust and if Einstein wouldn't have invented
the bomb, he might have been able to tie his shoes.
A vegetarian motorist sideswipes a junkfood pedestrian.
Someone kicks at the door yelling "The past is
my slave," but I'm out fishing for the water
to make the pond smaller for the big fish who
won't meet me halfway (as if the stars would burn out
were they not conscious of the constellations some
see them in). In math we learned two commandments
for every sense. The blackboard of the sky is erased
in a flash of sunrise only to be rebuilt as morning
and these flashes, these chances, these eyes
open wider than the mouth I mistake for my masculinity.

6.
The test patience and you flunk pretended to be life
as long as justice is counterfeit in the love derided
as right wing by the adolescent I'm hoping to be
recruited by a child in my war against.
You seemed content to cheat on me with what
you called my cute ass and I was content to pour
all my juice (pineapple) into the sink without drinking it
as an excuse to hike to the store for a new one,
because I had to see myself as a bad talker to listen
to you without having to read you as a self-help book
(unacceptable in the circles I move in, spinning my
wheels no doubt). And though it couldn't prevent me
from working at the villain factory as a paid volunteer
(feeling drafted), at least I could boast I wasn't
repulsed enough by you on an unconscious level
to idealize you on a conscious one.

7.

"But you," you said, "are but a flower proliferating
in a zone with no natural parasite but urban planning
pitifully underfunded as if there's no room for
ecology at the inn of economy & the rejected stone
becomes the corner stall of a church whose message
is tortured by the messenger unless dreams get in
the way and you try to cut them down because of
the cultural 'incentive' to 'write ourselves out of
Romanticism' (by, if not exactly sending students
to the country a la Mao, at least replacing the
emphasis on truth and beauty with an overemphasis
on "a" and "the")–which has luckily lost some of its
lustre, even in the evasive moods we're both suckers for."
So do you mind if I put you down as an emergency
contact, even though you fail to return my calls?

Storm Cloud Above the Swimming Pool

The waiting room is closed for the night.
The battle between birds who stand for signs
of sanity but fly into the branches so the tree
loses its footing and leaves those in the palace
(where everything is until it seems) guessing
and groping for a higher intimacy so sweet
all who touch it with lopsided willpower
slink back into the ooze they could only
leave on paper. No matter how convincingly
peaches fell from the trees of the past into
your stomach without reaching the mouth
of the present, the coffins of your "Only
so much god to go around" justice could
not prevent your bones from being moved
and you wake up with your legs twisted
because you fell asleep with your roots on.

She said "tell me everything" so excitedly
you didn't realize she meant "show me nothing."
But as long as I remain in doubt as to whether
speaking as a man to a woman is really speaking
to another man of the toilet he's the Tidy Bowl man of,
I may catch myself merely doing and loving what
the PR men of consciousness were so dead set against
since one can only live in the so-called moment
for so long, since your mistakes must make
the most-wanted list. If they're taken dead
you won't be able to kill them.
Of course, you don't want to.
But without the knowledge you could
all you'd know of love would be
the early haze of the first fall that, in winter,
you thought would be the last.

Functional Literacy (Disability Records)

To the extent doubt doesn't have to be seen
as a place in order to be lived in by one who
is surely an authority on the matter it loses itself in
until slapped on the face by a word or a bird
that keeps living on its toes, the loss which may
have to pass for love for the time being if one
is not to turn a slave to hate and the sparks
that fly more than they should are seen flunking
the test that flunks them, and we are at home
saying "there's no place like home."

But as long as personality becomes
a necessary medium through which to reveal
the tragic fate of moral truths, and showers
I only stood under when I stood for a duck
or at least its back in the great parlaiment of culture,
the speech that personified the wind, the hammer
that knocked it unconscious, took the winds out
of its sails, become the record that spins so fast
only a dog can hear the music in the people who
dance to the wags of its tail when they are pursued
by regret and guilt for the crimes against love
they are determined never to repeat again.

Party-Line Graffiti

The self-proclaimed cripple loses her case
When the defense shows a videotape of her
Wrestling in coleslaw. A mind made out of
Maxims refuses to relent, to air out
The body, or wash it in hunger.
You don't want to be cruel to the uprooted trees
You may share your bed with.
They have feelings too and just because
You cannot sing in tune with them
Is no reason to make a scene or break
A few dishes by singing a note so high
No human can hear it directly.
It is a note of joy, back when it was
Called the blues. It is the missing link
Edited out of every version of
The music of the spheres but those
Sung by dogs who have to drop a bone
To prick up their ears and shed
Their winter fur. Can we hear them
If we can't hear what they hear?

Can the full cry of the doctoral student
With the waggily tail still be heard
Amid the laughtrack of repression,
Holding onto dear life, disciples of winter,
As rodents emerge in the shadow of its dinosaur?
Revolutionaries asking us if we want a ride.
We do, of course, but from them?
What about our reputation?
What's love got to do with it?
Wouldn't be simpler if we could meet halfway,
If I didn't half to snowshoe over the Rockies
To get to you and find you've gone to hike
The more casual sedentary mountains

That are my habitual fictive backdrop?
Is it possible that no one called it a great divide
Until a golden spike was driven in
And freedom would not ring were not the bell cracked
And the "linty" flaws for which we stand
Become too easily sacred and I am scared
I trample on the memory you tremble.

Times like these when I wanna stalk
The superficial desires I doubt I can act on
Rather than the deeper ones I can
Only act on by doubting. I do not doubt
These desires. I only doubt that they are doubt
As a gap expands to be traversed by triggers
Firing bang flags which used to be as attractive
As nostalgia for the moist city surrounding me
Like a tongue reminding me of a grandmother
Gathering dandelions beneath the Brooklyn Bridge
For the soup of simplicity that gets
The last word on my attention deficit syndrome
Which is more easily condemned than killed.

How flattering, too, the photograph in which I am
A spider somersaulting into the jaws of his mate,
Or the one of us digging a garden and not counting
On any tomatoes or tomorrows in a world
Where we can only live hand to mouth which is
So easy to forget in a world of loans and savings
And ceilings that have to be looked at askew
To start snowing on my sofa! How flattering
To be pictured setting fire to every TV in town
(in hopes of being televised). And spending
My last good dollar on a wallet, I won my case
But lost it again in the kiln only a perverse clay
Would consent to be put in without the promise
Of eventual cooling. That may be how it started.
But in the oven the promises melt. Reason may

Airbrush the oven from the photograph.
But the photos, too, get thrown into the oven
Of our lovin' that cannot speak but if it could
It would certainly call reason treason for condemning
The gentleness only possible in lust
To the fast lane or fast track or flippered race
Up the stairs of the waterslide of conscious personality
The reruns of the rainbow may ravish more savagely
In boy meets girl cranberry *chalance.*

A stillness seems to slow down,
Present division sees past manyness as one
In the rearview mirror not yet shattered enough,
Not yet off enough to be on. It was a thrill to strip
For the blind woman, to let ghosts fondle me and
Stencil Party Line Graffiti on every straightforward
Hearse harpooned into the waiting room, lassoed
By a once in a lifetime highschool, and be plopped
Like a tornado into a hospital amazed by
My own solidity, a flipside not played
Until the sea recedes and the bicyclists arrive
Before the motorists to the senses seen as censors
To those with saunas they wish to proffer
As thick (political) skins.

What others regard as my virtues I no longer regard virtuously
Until the Honda I've never seen (yours)
Pulls into the interstate driveway of my thoughts
And lets me commit more crimes of desire
As if I am a priest blessing the house and demanding
The money you wouldn't know what to do with
Without me. The blessing goes something like this:
"What good is the flag that signifies freedom
if you can't burn it? What good is democracy
if we can't all be tyrants? What good is a castle
unles it's made of sex? And what good is sex
if it's not a form of tribute, a structure that can be sold,
but, if felt intensely, could eventually sell away the store?"

Nothing can hold you, even abstractions would whine
Were they not too busy cancelling each other out
To lead my tongue to your eyebrow and telling it
Not to lick, as if acknowledged cruelty is easier
To manage than the frightened floaters we become
In floods of money paving the future with fragments
To clog up the flow. Passion is play's only populists
And delight only becomes terror to ward off the filth
Of philosophy, the mischief of belief, from the land
Of laughter and forgiveness I need more faith in
Like I need a hole in my head. If we can meet in the oven
Where palaces are tenements, each flick of fortune's finger
May roll a fling around us like a red carpet to crown the sea
Without killing it by establishing pure madcap sex zones
Between the embarrassed world trade tower legs
Of an ex who wanted to dance on my nose
(But I guess I'll carry on, even if you fail to call my bluff).

Love for Money, Food for Thought

The nagging theme of balance...
The possibility you could make her impossible.
If I have to tell them to be with you,
if I have to fly from California to La Guardia
to get to Oklahoma, I will.
Will body language take up the slack
once the words are seen slacking off?
Or is it in its power to fire them?

So I crash the party of phony patience and
"there goes the neighborhood" is all the thanks I get.
I try giving up hope for her. The hope that made me
too impatient for worldly success. Misogyny?
Just because I invite that interpretation doesn't mean
I embrace it. Nor do I need to expand my circle
or dredge up the user friendly fire of memory.
It's enough that I have to be in 3 hours.
At least something nearby's open 24
and they may sell lightbulbs and adapters
to allow fence-sitters the illusion of fencing,
the broom that sweeps you up in things
even before you pay...

There is something you don't have to sit
as still as all that to pay attention to,
a stillness closer to dancing than stiffness,
something you have to dance to pay attention to
and the pregnant woman dances too.
I go about trying to put the future into the now,
as one only learns the grammar of his native tongue
by living a second. Without a second,
the first is nothing. Without a future
the present is nothing. Without symbolic import
the image is nothing. We go in and out

of each other. No breaks are clean
but seem so at first.

The walrus throws another party and I go
for the Hungarian physics major & the possibility
of matchmakers stapling mistletoe onto
the convertible top that'll surely be up
since the forecasters are all rooting for
the rainy day I've been saving up for
now that I've been rerouted to accept
the working weak who tell me I'm a lover
not a writer and give the weekend meaning.

Because the job allows neither love
nor thought, they're pushed like rival tribes
westward onto reservations. Bunched up,
the debate over the virtues of killing each other off.
As strange bedfellows, they'll make the best
of bad situations without the nagging fear
that the government will see how happy they are
and because of that deny them what they
would have gotten if only they had rioted.

No, you don't heal others by becoming sick.
"But I was sick to begin with," you may protest,
"and so have nothing to lose." Sure, you were
born crying (if I may so presume) in a land
where feeling's beaten out of you so gently
you didn't notice. The wailing of original sin.
Yet just 'cause the church (across the hall
from the kung-fu studio) I made $20
playing "Climb Every Mountain" (their choice)
and "Redemption Songs" (my choice) in
doesn't believe in original sin doesn't mean
I'm gonna join it. I know something that must
be wrestled with to be loved, but that doesn't mean
I'll go scraggly for just anyone.

Photo: Copyright © Star Black, 1998

Chris Stroffolino was born on March 20, 1963—the same day Allen Ginsberg wrote "Death News"—in Reading, Pennsylvania, where he lived (aside from a six month stint in Washington serving on the staff of two failed Presidential candidates) until he received his B.A. in English/Philosophy from Albright College in 1986. He received a M.A. in English from Temple University in 1988 and a Ph.D. in English from SUNY-Albany in 1997. Stroffolino has taught English on an adjunct level at Rutgers University, Long Island University, Touro College, The University of Massachusetts, Peirce Junior College and Drexel University. He has also worked as a factchecker, proofreader, newsclipper, videostore clerk, gallery assistant, waiter, sandwich maker, janitor, security guard and his piano playing can be heard on the Silver Jews' *American Water* LP (Drag City, 1998). He currently lives in New York City.

lingo books

Home In Three Days. Don't Wash.
Linda Smukler

little men
Kevin Killian

Tilt
Gillian McCain

No Both
Michael Gizzi

White Thought
Tom Clark

Blow
Lynn Crawford

The Letters of Mina Harker
Dodie Bellamy

Half Angel, Half Lunch
Sharon Mesmer

Stealer's Wheel
Chris Stoffolino

Series Editor: Jonathan Gams